asked
what has
changed

wesleyan poetry

*

ALSO BY ED ROBERSON

When Thy King Is a Boy (1970)

Etai-eken (1975)

Lucid Interval as Integral Music (1984)

Voices Cast Out to Talk Us In (1995)

Just In: Word of Navigational Challenges: New and Selected Work (1998)

Atmosphere Conditions (2000)

City Eclogue (2006)

The New Wing of the Labyrinth (2009)

To See the Earth Before the End of the World (2010)

Closest Pronunciation (2013)

ED ROBERSON

asked
what has
changed

Wesleyan University Press
Middletown, Connecticut

WESLEYAN UNIVERSITY PRESS

Middletown CT 06459

www.wesleyan.edu/wespress

Manufactured in the United States of America

Designed and typeset in Fresco Plus Pro

by Eric M. Brooks

Library of Congress Cataloging-in-Publication Data

NAMES: Roberson, Ed, author.

TITLE: Asked what has changed / Ed Roberson.

DESCRIPTION: Middletown, Connecticut : Wesleyan University Press, [2021] |

SERIES: Wesleyan poetry | Summary: "Intertwining sharp yet nuanced
   reflections on the natural world with images of urban landscapes,
   environmental crises, and political issues, the poet depicts a world of
   connectivity, continuity, and transformation"— Provided by publisher.

IDENTIFIERS: LCCN 2020038900 (print) | LCCN 2020038901 (ebook) |
   ISBN 9780819580108 (cloth) | ISBN 9780819580115 (trade paperback) |
   ISBN 9780819580122 (ebook)

SUBJECTS: LCGFT: Poetry.

CLASSIFICATION: LCC PS3568.O235 A93 2021 (print) | LCC PS3568.O235 (ebook)
   | DDC 811/.54—dc23

LC record available at https://lccn.loc.gov/2020038900

LC ebook record available at https://lccn.loc.gov/2020038901

5 4 3 2 1

contents

asked
what has
changed

asked what has changed

Even staring out the window is changed,
the private peak above it all brought down
with the erosion of the poise between
the viewable and the mused unseen.
Dissolution so nearly changeless as not
to appear is shifting the sands inside
from what we watched, no more the steady stage
the self-dramatic days play out on   outside.
The silent portent now allowed alert
to things changing   the light
                              a darkness
not the normal individual
mortality, but as if the epochal
heartbeat of larger elements, the seas,
the air, had mutated, become chimera,
grown wing, and routed ancestral time.
Even staring out the window, the timeless
is gone. We see coming
in the daily migration of the local geese
to the lake at evening   the cities pull up
and move   in unlike consternation towards and
                              away from the water
that had been so calming to gaze out on,
to live by, easy   to not live according to.
And now that seas are adding themselves
into the land, horizons look ominously larger,
the arrivant out of them, faster and clearer.
Now, you see the view is turned on us to frame
human agency become transparent,

light as air, before the picture blackens
as a consequence of our seeing too much
of it as only for us   to use and then

                                 use up.
The eye is not filled with seeing, with only
seeing, but with understanding the sight.

a drop of water

*

From the window the surface of the puddles
says it's raining   you can't see it falling
in the street lights or the darkened windshield
wipers' smoothing it away

The silver of wetness has been steady
for days   crows' feathers
have been the light composition
of the streets   un-phased they eat

and don't fly away at the light
exposing their dark plate   until the last
minute   not to become timeless themselves
they are the droplets of lightning that return upward

screaming at the disturbance
jumping up and down on the surface of everything
that matters   troubling
the structure of even the structure-less

water   water   so it is water
not rain
though it only changes its name
even though it clearly says trouble

I don't know what it is
I'm seeing

(I'm seeing . . .)

my liquid body   water in a flesh glass
on the dining car table as the train crosses
a track change   the surface of the water
appears as ripples untouched by any stone

oscillating in place   or as
when my friend quietly says that
is an aftershock   or what I've heard
music sets up

off the walls of our body
structures that hang
in our blood   and show that
standing at a bus stop

when not the one I want rumbles through
the potholes   I can feel
my body floating up and down
and know   there is nothing under my feet

but another street I can't see
the engineering
translates the suspension
to me   what reception is triggered

by this signal   I don't know what I am yet
making of what is called troubling

(what is called troubling . . .)

the water.
what has changed from glancing out at the weather
to the unrevealed information held in
the pointillist flux of water   raising

something in me   a back jet   a levitating globule
is a deepening in everything
I want to know   the larger networks
of answers' ripple —

flowering   the trees   the loam they're loomed from
the earth   that pops
free of its drop   as itself a moment
for a glimpse   before

resolution back into the pool.
the idea being that if
our reality is holographic,
that bubble   blanket-tossed up

above the ripple's circle is us
where   on it I am following these images
the same way   to here
resolved into a juggling fool

whose water oranges round up one
morning come off the horizon of the lake as sun.

$(\ldots)$

The wind making the surface ripples
on the pool at Bethesda is said to be
the voice of God passing.   get its
attention   ask a question   it's not certain

what happens   it's not certain with anything
that happens   what exactly did.
if some exactitude was even agent
or those dice the brain said didn't exist did —

those ripples   the drop's crown on acceptance
an ebullient earth leapt up
whether to look about   or a rebellion
free   in a violent moment —

one morning you will recognize the sun
a face that has no assurance you see
on it that it sees anything   especially
none pertaining particularly to you

that answer   that the sun comes up tomorrow
doesn't even take your question.

after

After the press conference in the garden
everything seemed to grow silent   silently
the green fuse was not heard to charge the flowers
with any song from their trumpets   any

choral response to answer.   ?   —   amen.
The squash blossom simply got gainfully
green filled our mouths with shut up louder
than stomach's basic unfilled line of inquiry,

as if once answered no question next mattered.
But next   is time   is life   is you after
the heads cut off their broadcast   and you must eat
the suicide fish with the venom   expertly chef-removed   sweet.

And any hymn sung   is to you who eat
having learned how to prepare your leaders.

first person

This time not one apple but how many
we think we can force to market,   our mistake
fallen in line,   a snake that deceives us
into bankruptcy and collapse,   our bellies
to the ground,   the market of creation down.

Since it turned out the names were not names
but recipes, the table has been the point
of communion with the earth —
eat the ground's cover down to the dirt,
pull the meat out of the air, pop the pod surface
of the waters for the last bean of fish,
eat fire, energy until only ashes are left.

And the mind, maybe the fifth element —
eat it   like when the mind eats its familiar
when it fails to be the other persons
of itself it is in the whole collective
world of other eyes,   otherwise,   in other
words,   it eats itself.

A world that runs out on   runs out of   itself dies,
our idea of ourselves as apart from everything else
has eaten us out of house and home,
is eating away at me inside.

the way we are

The way we are   with this everything is ours
to use up   when we took over everything
our proprietary space disappeared
it was up   like everything   over
for grabs it was gone out   of existence
by definition   say   used up is us as

it seems to have been our nature
to avoid defining ourselves as
a running out even though we have death
as our exemplar   we used that up
as god the user up imagined
his fill like our gut   not its rot

satisfied   this is the satisfaction
we are facing   the using up of paying up

the land

*

In one of the cross-connecting streets
there are concrete urns you can half sit
or lean on   the city keeps filled with plants

and branches in seasonal arrangements
paced down the block.   I don't turn
onto this street   it turns on me   it approaches.

I am grateful city workers make a living
doing this to me   each of the me walking
down this street.   How do we each return this?

Is there ever any one tree in the city of trees
that is the forest one can thank for the green
stroll through the shade opening to the sun?

No one to hear   because each stroller *is* the city.
One prays a vote with a full feel of the arrangement.

In one of the cross-connecting streets
curbs parked with those nowhere to go,
the storefronts idle   fruitless and withered   grow

the banks' financially zoned arrangements
branches of dead trees in the lots.

Old lead-painted window ledges at
just that height to look out   to bite on
because children want something in their mouth.

I don't turn onto this street   because it can turn on me
its howling reflex of stepped on   its history
it turns on me my government's police gunshot

when I am unarmed and haven't done anything
returning home   how do I return   This unwelcome
arrangement   is The Land   that connects this street to the city.

the street knows it's changed

*

The street knows it's changed   its direction.
once it was here now it's the way to
someplace else   benches had been waiting
to catch the little talk that got off
and gathered at that corner
now there is standing timed
for as little the mobile app schedules
tolerate safely   limiting arrival
to one if any anticipatory
glance down the road except for what's late
as little weather to wait with as neighbor
known by name   the temperatures
all strangers to this time of year here
now   now is known to be looking elsewhere.

speculation

*   *. . . Tyger, Tyger*

what comes after the ocean where it is
what will move in
what kind of neighborhood will it bring

what is that familiar horizon packing up
      selling off or getting rid of we don't see
      out on the curb
what can it not pull out and have to leave
      in place in the sky

what if nothing moves in after the ocean
what will that   absentee profit's
      crackheads   look like
what will they do to get it

what will there be to be got
if oh no
what will there be to beget

who can hold on to lifeless property
      and how be that rich   for millennia
where will the artsy gentrifiers come from
who can pay these prices

outlook

*

Tore pages from the TIAA-CREF annual report
to stuff the cracks around the window mounting
of the air conditioner. I catch numbers
in the hundreds of thousands stuffed in the columns
of print. My pension is a whiff of that.
The hawk comes through the cracks so hard
the blinds rattle.

This is what lists as a luxury apartment in the South Side
a 75 year old national register early international style
hi rise upper floor view landscaped grounds heat
35 mph winds inside   view.   I can see the lake,
rim of horizon size pitcher, source of Chicago's smelly tap water.
Industries and water-starved communities as far as out west
have their eyes on this

single source of fresh water to fill their pockets.
Their eyes on this the same as on those neighborhoods
needed   out of their way   or working for them   those
who have all the money. This itself always dispersed
through the drift of some field error, some miscalculation.
Or simply time, its eye on everything. The hawk comes through the cracks
so hard the blinds rattle.

the corner unit

*

The corner unit
— over and down into the lake —

of the apartments
in the building

is in both
the lake and the land

worlds as well
as up in the sky —

the heavy liners of the scheduled
geese in their straightaway

and the crazy
swallows   the gull's white ballet —

from the balcony
this is city

living at its
most ethereal.

east across the water
and north across the residential

roofs and trees into
the line of skyscraper cliffs.

The toes of the clouds hang down
rain shafts   the earth sucks

up in a dance —
the rivers' orgasmic unraveling

roots fly up and curl
around a harvest flushed across the skin

of the fields
the routes of migration

following the woman who is food
the river goddesses of spread

it around and trade rosette knots
of their pubic hairs'

lines in the genealogies
of cultural epic —

from the mortal earthly rail,
the stop closest to Riverwalk   somewhere out there

what is city living
from the most mortal and earthly   where

is that view taken
from.

documentation

You have to be up high yourself
to notice how far the shadows
of the tall reach across the water

the skyscrapers lying out
into the lake   wharves for
the incoming from another

angle from which reflection is cast
a different line of docking the world

to see people walking off a plane
that in another was water —

the only mystery not being able
to explain the tilt   but recognizing there

days I could feel the slant
and see nothing.

fallen open on the statue's lap

*

A white news-page of snow fallen
open on the statue's lap   waits
reading   while my edition bakes
glacier and volcano all in one

flow.   Unlike old news.   Neither really
wanted what we already knew
nor too new   a range we're used to
now we've this news big as all history —

But rivers flow and mountains rise
melted ice or cindered stone read
as what they weren't supposed to   mean
an almost nothing   can change everything

to writing on water   life on fire
Pompeian cast figures   reading   air

alley, here we name them "way"

*

Cart and horse scaled streets, some US cities have
Alleys couched enough   that way the British might say mews.
Doors silent the size to walk through,
For delivery, not to interrogate your journey,
Not big mouthing in stasis the importance
Of their place, ready to say not your
Destination;   but here, actually someone's home   in the alley.

The neighborhood is changing
People are moving in as out
Faster than we can see who is
Going to be here,   who the violence will leave
Unclear,   who unafraid.

A street scale   without moving I could talk across
A line of words as easily as walk
To hand you some of the first fresh ripe
Tomatoes I'd hosed clean because I know
You're going to bite right there into one   your way
To let me know you think I know
How to live   across the street, across a way

A way to   as in dance say   step come to   agree
Destination in peace,   the route differing
For finishing together on one note.
The flourish of that last corner's twirled collision
That has no one thrown off the word for his land.

These places have a quiet unprotected reputation
So cheap   a way to run out   with city-cleaning out his alley,
Out of his way of doing run
Out of others' way who don't that way   do things like
Run them out —

A street the scale of what is happening instead
Of others' want,   a street scaled to let help to what's here
get through.   Get.
      A way.

deer scare: answer with missing riddle

*

A bell with short chops for its ring
Shock
        where are due the praise
fancyings of bronzes singing
        there is hollow wood
The tock talk of bamboo

        The hours like deer
        frightened away

*

what could it have sounded like to the deer
of those who invented it as   time keeper
and alarm   and to which of them   and whether
it is even time   and of which to fear,

maybe it's   the sound that which is hollow makes
maybe it is toppling   or any imbalance
or not understanding what mechanism is
set off to make this sharp start happen,

or maybe a rock-sparked wood ignites
a fire we   who have not had to run from as long don't know
— some dream of a garden awakening
awake in flame

as this garden   alerted to what we know
mightn't set us free this time in time   to use it.

trace

    The smooth alluvial floor of a cave
in the riverbank, a lean-to temporary

only on the geological scale of the lilting
cliff on a dial, the tacky clay

ready for the stylus of a bird's foot,
is cool and quiet in its shade.

    Usually it's the present's loud initials
scratching into the walls by hand or collision,

pointing the way in its tracks or trailing
the prey prophesy of an eye across the hand to the wall

and over —   while the great concavity of sky overhead
mirrors a heron mist standing over water,

    the earth swimming by in its shade.
into range.

The long time of light about
to become its flash we record as star

written in water,
that fish in the heron's shadow   a minute is.

the insect *ephemera*

*

The insect *Ephemera* has a life
of only hours   the rose fades   a cloud
only holds its shape a matter of seconds
The lightness of the transitory gone
with its day   is not what we feel
when we contemplate extinction   though
their forevers are the same   disappearance

We return a past from the ruin reduced
to a few articulate stones   or an impression
left from a step through a mud flat
or we feel an emotion wring us out of a song
or story   the recorder   its kind   long gone —
Something has leapt the disappearance
back into existence   some consistent

information able   to reformulate itself
in a receiver set to get it —
the shellac roll   the wax the vinyl
disc the tape the film the light numbers
and the box —   will there be a box under the tree
who will unpack it   set it up   do they know
what listening is

is there a female
did anyone pack the poems

morello's venice

*

startled to hear the doctor say
this would be the last time he would see it,
a person used to keeping things alive
talking terminus —   even more

startled when he returned
to hear him say it wasn't there
there were terrible rains
bookings cancelled.

when late he arrived,
everything was gone.
his wife had a cold.

they bundled together in blankets.
he refilled my prescription to
restore my soul.

a way of seeing as deep as the sea
is   a drunkenness of seeing

when the wine talks   the walls wash away
we see   the colors of the changes   through

the consequential meaning   we thought
was the eye of god   it was just

the ending   the surface disappearing
then blank   the transparency to say   what we see —

Venice without canals.
only water.

his song is the wine dark sea
her eyes are the wine dark sea —

when they wash ashore   out of their mouths spills
the wine dark sea.

the empty of the bottlenecks

*

What happens
is that which happens without what we know of it.

Paris without Notre Dame happened two weeks ago
Persepolis was gone again three years ago.

We have pictures again
We think this just may be the last.

Venice without the canals
Only water.

Only a Chicago size huddle of us left
on the face of the earth

no New Delhi no New York Mexico City Los
Angeles ever again   all that down

to a Chicago size huddle of us left scattered across
the face of the earth.

It has
happened before.

We can
never be sure

which time
will be

able to
continue

only
to no

more
than none

no size no
huddle to happen.

the child in fellini's *satyricon* bacchanal scene
   *

Seated at the balcony of the fourth wall   of the world
staring over/ at   the wall   as if the world
                     the handwriting on the wall   as if Venice
                     the audience

the audience feels him looking at them
maybe wondering   who are these people looking at
                                             us
the audience feels   who are these people (on stage)
                          looking at   / like   us

If the child is
    visualizing   us/ being watched   an objective perspective
    reading   the writing on the wall

then the audience should feel themselves
                              in.

    the aspect of the child
                        reading   the writing on the wall

The child is the young god of objective perspective
                            grapes in his hair

                         present at
                         but ignored because it/
                         he   has not matured

come about   yet
inherited the consequence

we/   the audience
are ignored   by the events   the happenings   by the stage
                                                                   on stage now

The Morellos at the Hotel

                                                                   as if the poem.

the hold of extinction

*

a feeling is over   once the nerve calms —
a sight is seen   once it puts you in position —
and you   self subjective regime
look over it   to something else —

but some little bastard keeps his records
and the shout goes on sale again as a different
play in another city scape   new instrumentation —
what disappears gets into the walls   and its echoes

take shapes   the scientists say   the atmosphere
leaves its impressions on rock   the weight of air
is there   eternities later   to be read
as anything it wants.   number   spectrometric color

climatic epic of hot and cold —   the
jar!   Pouring itself into its emptiness   the deep hold

the listening

*

We always think we are
listening from a distance —

but in a state where the wildfires
move eighty-three feet per minute

we might not be fast enough
to outdistance events

anymore   we can go up
in a puff prior to any announcement.

Up in smoke
                        used to mean disappeared
but half the state   useless   though it

is is   still here
the poisonous smoke   settling back

to the blank ground
that cataract   it all went over.

millimeters of corneal tissue

*

x millimeters of the y number of centimeters of
the surface of your living
organism   structures what that organism experiences
living in.

Within the periphery of that
field of vision emanating from so few millimeters of receptor
you contain Lake Michigan
you can see across to the three geographically adjoining states

from the top of the John Hancock
building up to the question
of what you saw that led you up there.

What in those cells' respondent construction
of this   space shall we call it   produced you following
up   a hundred stories of steel

What in the world were you picking up
— and putting down   apparently —   those footings
what were they
imagining they had to hold up —

and what of the rest of your living
organism's surface in contact with
out itself   is inside
resonating with what it is   within, vibrating

out of some music   a respiratory breathing   a heart
out of some tide   a call of return
out of some ether of astronomy   our own aural calculation.

What in these placeless points   figures what we show up at —
whether it's a visionary evolution,
or an extinction.

light on the threshold

*

When you live high in the mountains
your foundation is the sky   not the ground
on which you lay your feet —   that is like a shelf
or side-table top to hold your tools.

What you are working on is the sky.
It is the walls you watch to protect you
It is the surface on which you hang
the sketches of your inventions   to erase

like wind and correct by survival.
It is the art you are thinking you want to see
up there   the foundation
of your sofa and chairs' arrangement

where you settle after dinner   and unbutton
her blue blouse of a painting before bed.

On the two-lane mountain roads where the buses go over
the sides   a thousand feet down   regularly —
when you come to a sharp curve you can't
see around   you are out over the valley

not on the ground for a time.   Out there.
where it is all figuring which house
of the next moment will stand   on its nothing
there.   Here, living on the fifteenth floor

up   close to the lake   light in Chicago
the white window sill floats — ceiling
to knee-high open glass   the white reflecting the sky
out there   into the apartment.

Let me open your blouse   let me, the air
in   to brush the dust off all your sill.

_____

OE *syll*: threshold

sand

*

The sand sticks to me as though it had fallen
as snow   the silica's wet glitter   dry.

I am coated with a line as if I had lain
in water   floating like the boats that lie

about what they are on   in the glare —
sky and water interchanging their light.

I am uncertain what luminary
bears this sandcastle illusion upright.

This beach wasn't here before the hurricane,
houses that were here aren't here either.

The glaciation of this earth-change planes
away the known in the thin curl we feared

it was
something we brush off that could be brushed off.

wine-dark sea

*

The amount of water a blue whale must feel
along its skin from its nose to its tail

a hundred feet away   must fill
an Olympic size pool of thought.

The thought of a pool left in the rocks
by the receding tide holds my reflection.

The oceanic glaze of the planet paints all this
a hot minute on a hot rock

In a cold sky   cloud mists
of star   galaxies —

Inches from my fingertips   a cold drink
the thin slice of a spherical lime

wheels a glorious drunkenness.   Does the whale
feel the whole ocean, the planet   roll off it?

To roll the ocean, the planet   off one's skin —
that crayon moving along what it holds on

to as surface   hews the eye cavity
with what it sees   the deep valleys

of fingerprint with what its handling identifies,
the soaring peaks of feeling with more

than a carried down name.   A fractal meaning of hand
to hand.   The cup

of looking into it all swallowing   being
drunk down.

Crossing what we do   looping our cursive crazy through
the us of it all we are taking in   we are drinking

more than the simple ocean   more
than the amount of water a blue whale must feel.

the universal ephemeral

A universe of so much of

       I'm sure
time   would like to know what a moment is
other than its one   The umbilicate ear
-shaped galaxy listening to one   drop

of sudden afternoon   rain beneath the eaves
in one of the backwash summer eternities
I'm sure it would like to duck into that

off time   ducked into centuries,   a dark age, a Macy's
and shopped   whole histories a diversion
dropped

       when the sky clears up —
limit's detail   lived   as all there is
and the whole of that   lived as the all their ones,
both at once and wholly aware they are

done an entire time   we live
as   ever.

mutable point of axis

*

Submerged leaves in the invisible flow
over the settlements of the stream bed,
as smooth a counter-cross of movement as aircraft
seen passing below the altitude we're at

forward but sideways and seen faster than they are,
as in a maelstrom of motions, the two almost
pinned to spin on an axis of our passing,
crossing over intersecting aircraft below

throws it around behind you before it goes under
and disappears.   When we placed the gods overhead
it didn't occur this is where they'd see   from: that point,
where from above,   moving   directions appear nonsense.

Just as here,   that isn't newspaper either
rolling across the park lawn,   it's a garbage of gulls
well above ground level but below
the view from these upper floors,   blown

gray wings the day's edition,   pages I didn't
go downstairs to pick up at the newsstand
that now fly by   out of my hands —
as beyond my grasp as those   scheduled

crossings of planes   as of the gods' said
crossing of plains
of war   or of lovers' stars.

mutable point of access

*

Above a certain floor I think we pay
　　a few dollars more for the exalted
view.
　　It's just a block square lawn bordered
with trees
　　then a square mile of undeveloped re:
development, razed, failed; an open
　　　　　　　　　　　　　　　　walled
by a major thruway in, against the wall
of the city.
　　　　　It doesn't matter from the ground
you can't see it, we who do imagine
no more
　　　　than its openness　　a paradise
we look down on　　from.

to those who would skate the larger surface

*

Cold, new-metal bright, the December air
seems to have cleared the streets,
though the season has not seen a flake of snow;
and what over-again used Christmas hung
already feels like left over street side parking signs
for sweeping.   Subtly backwards.
Our equipment at a confused ready is
one of the milder changes we are told to expect.

A drop, local now,   of a great waterfall ahead.
Look for territories to change,   an Arctic owl this south
to fumble its catch of an American coot and drop it dead
among the Christmas night ice skaters in the park.   They all
fall down.   Pile-ups on roads that hardly move
the temperature one way or the other, snowed under.
Not breezes we simply sit and catch, but have to
dig out, splint our arms and homes, and mop out the holiday

instead.   The dead coot, bloodied broken neck
dropped on the time's skaters,   draws down the season.
The haunt white moon of circling owl wing glows
a way through   the turning out of the lights.   The shifts
of territories   of rains   the bloom lines of food   re-corridor
movement where the predators,   already hungry,   wait.
People are walking in their socks, their skates, shoes with what little
time they had to take them off   on   over their shoulders.

the old homology

*

The upper body of the sphinx rests on
its elbows and forearms outstretched,
it can lean its lower body forward between
the peaks of pointed knees if we think of these

structures like our own   except in a cat.
Knees and elbows   or a gazelle.

What is a foreleg but the joined extended
bone of palm from the wrist to a single
fingernail, a hoof   to which we draw a likeness?

The homologous menageries we first see in clouds
are the starter toys of creativity:
To see a like, to make a match, to mind

a child starving near death sits
on his haunches   on the ground nearly the same
silhouette as the waiting patience
of a vulture keeping its crouched distance feet away.

eye ear nose and throat

*

They stopped listening the same time they learned
speaking more   than the grunt call who where they were;
they stopped hearing at a distance with their eyes,
knowing the light's vibrations through the soles of feet
that drummed what would become signal said outside,
word   rather than the knowing finely recognized
in a collective attention as what
then became singular to each, a voice to say.   Run!

And they no longer share mind, this humankind
became dumb to us. They could no longer smell
what they now say,   and spoken to through air
they only think what someone is watching   is them.
They are beyond what is animal says
to them.   Their world must be a husk of inward absence,
            the peeled off as words.
            Their world a husk of peeled off word
            must be a kernel of innermost silence
                        deeper than stars
                        they listen at now for
                                    language

eco echo etude

Cat   the plump palm of her
          paw   for handling
distance's reach
          of   sound
is   the softest piano
          foot
                    pedal

while the toe of my fingers
traces   in the white whisper grain
          of sails
a mute lake
dangling from the appearance
                    jutting out into
a waving   grass   flow
to the horizon
                    and walks on paper
                    water.

The plumb of our likeness
          our animal
territorial scratch on the bark of this
plant transformed as it is to paper

        audiences   which is to say
makes to hear   responses to the homologous
in the chance of birds attending
        song

in the chance
of   poetry   to attend
        imagination
's song

                    audiences
                    verb present   sing
                    see   listens   as something else.
                                                 to study

loco moveri

*

Antelope don't
look like they put their feet
down on anything;

they seem to pick at
the ground, to pinch
themselves off

the ground up into air;
whereas horses seem to dig at
to scoop away the distance.

The wheel almost never lifts
to miss a measure, but that song
has no organic round

of evolution it has won
unless   in a long lost sea —
or that roll

of the foot flat
part not whole of the wheel
our own   a broken tape on the ground.

Is this why we sing through
these death marches? Measure?
Calling out

to each other to keep up
to not get picked off,
touch the fellow footstep as

all that's sound of the earth
and to know where to go   silent
traceless when we steal away and run on the wing.

sense

Out in the clouds, the panicked herd of heat
lightning gallops back and forth corralled
into a sky fenced by earth into
everywhere overhead.
                       The animal
at the grounded mercy of what it can't hear
but is coming   underneath the audible.

The smell before storms that raises those hairs,
the ears.   That lifts your head out of the crowd
before the nose even catches on.
                         A wind
of which you can't see,   of what if anything
there   except answer a full leap ahead of
any question,
                an alertness
that runs you last
to die.

for Kenny

kingfisher

*

Glimpse something drop   like fruit from a branch
of trees along the river   then fall back
up to its perch —   you've caught the kingfisher
burst from its dive,   back   into position
over the water,   nearly invisible reign;
Or just as explosively,   a stillness
pop out of the background   a blue — heron.

Watching brings them   into being but for
their own coalescence   out of nothing
to do with us   any more than us with
them.   Interdependence   a scribbling
outside the lines   of what   we know to draw.
The sharpened quill   only closer draws itself
a feather   shaft to branch to barb and hook,

but never finally   fine enough to
nothing   between the wing and thin air
edges are   not the limit we thought.
Name outside itself,   of the subject hid
in itself   into its own pattern with   the ground,
the living eye must translate: diamond back
the stripe the spotted light   shadow into sight

back from nested camouflage   in the whole
of indeterminacy   back into flight
inside the lines   of time to stay itself
alive.   Where to step.   An underground
railroad guide's read.   tree or face.
Take Smuggler's Notch   the last leg to Canada.
You can see down the climb for a day who's behind you   and
        there are caves   to fade into or appear
        out of   free

swallows are making the sky crazy

*

    not the louvered flocking of a school
or finned seabirds   nor the plotted squall
of pigeons over a coast of roofs,   not the V
and line of the geese arrow,   rather

swallows fly   with that insect erratic
feeler for ahead   of their buzz targets,
they crawl all over the sky   bugs over each other
in as many directions as their complex eyes;   see

locked here in the focus of the window,
the swallows are making the sky crazy,
the crackle glaze that their flight fires on the air
dares sky to fall tinkling to the ground

— rain, a snow of stars, the shattering Judgment
or an ancient bowl's perfected whole
of silence —   for that instant their flight holds
in place   at first glance before seeing it move.

See the wheel stand still before it turns
to introduce the spoke before it blurs away,
the hours before their speed through our hands,
and when ours end,   retain the after image

of memory.   why make anything between   such scribble
the swallows are making,   the sky crazy?

cascade

*

Standing at the window   suddenly to my left
   I caught the cascade   down the face of the building
of a flock of starlings   disappear below me

in that motion   I could have been   standing beside
   a waterfall midway   the drop of a rollercoaster
built off a hill   into a hollow

following   birds the eye rides
   I'm up the opposite air   my arms above my head
air-time in cloud.

My daughter says she can tell   when I drive
   west across Pennsylvania   when I feel
I'm home   Yes, I can feel   the landscape driving
           the hills curving the road

discovering   on her baby nap inducing afternoon
   drives we took by the canal   my daughter kept awake
until we crossed a rise   she had a secret name for

*the road hump monste*r   who reaches up
   to grab your stomach   just as you drive over.
I thought that her   *Faster Daddy!*

was to her like the lift into the air-   toss dads enjoy
   once we get over   being afraid we'll drop her.
But it was another stone of trust   fall into place
   It was the grab of ground we all fear more much later I'd got her over

Once she'd taught me where the monster lives   there are times
    I can feel him staring   like someone seated opposite
on the bus   I look and he turns away

is how people feel   another person's eyes
    on them   that someone is staring and react
like grabbing the strap   on a curve with only

the muscle body   without the thinking
    through the potholes   the peoples jarred by them speak up
not *Faster*   Damn! cussing the city,   the one more   death
    of a child shot by another,   that reach of the street.

Motion in space   up or down   looked
      across   is a sensation   the feel of how far
you can see   experienced   with the visioning physical body

as with the equalizing steer
      you stare against the pull of sight   lines to stay you in your lane
drawn to a summer dressed beauty   in your same direction

that shared   seeing feelings as words
      making up their stories   the whole car would lean into.
But even at still   a motion

drawn as by magnetic line   of concentration
      a gravity turns your head   to its no one staring
in the quick   look   but programmed guidance of

hunted survival   we measure in muscle still what's there
      instantly travelled through   the eye
physical body of sight   brushes

down the face of the building
      in that motion
my arms up the opposite air   sky time kinks off my hair
      infinite spirals   fire   toward the black hole's center.

color change

*

A yellow vw seen across the lot
through the changing leaves
is driven paler by their yellows turning stranger,

as if in terror at the bare blinded sense
the winter makes of fickle foliage,
of oil and anti-freeze demands, the tires . . .

Were birds damned all one color, they would change
like leaves, but they change places, and the absence
stands out as miraculous against what stays.

The cardinal and its first   fresh snow,   that seasonal
form of water   are the bud of a world   more halting
than all reds,   able to bring those crystals' six-sided stream

to a standstill of translucent blue-green stone.
Yet its glacier too is migratory in a dying sun's yellowing down

dawn . . .   A simple reduction to its colors going out
of meaning   its meaning something else in that location
opens me to the chemical residue through which what continues

articulates.   A beautiful redhead
the particular vibration continues
its measure as red   that she is black   Jamaican

without such counting or counter disappears
back into continual background space
the stars such an observer had seen as heaven.

But vibrations encountered rise or lower
into other dimensions   a rock
capable of aluminum oxide   corundum   maybe never

to be called ruby   or *kuruvinda*
an untranslatable state of luminat being.

luxe

You should wonder what the necklace of your
fingernails and teeth look like worn
for instance   by the bear that ate you   more

likely than not   very unpolished   or
a cave wall hanging
                            too skinny   rug even
peeled open for the floor,
                                      more belts and wallets
were bears enamored of accessories,
what with the sun-bleached tip of each hair

to flop back and forth through their fur
an iridescence   wind-like through a field,

how redundant you are in addition,
useless   if aesthetics have no nutrient,

but then   you might not even have a beauty
to collect, have anything to do with anything except
                                    the way you see

You should wonder what a necklace of your teeth
would bring among the animal trade
                                             your ears
war criminals among your own were known
to string like cowries
                        of victory   your genitals
in jars on desks your conquerors kept
to terrify their sharecroppers —
                              but animals
don't keep containers outside their bodies
as their mess;
               you should wonder what your bones
drape like in their stomachs
                              what your eyeballs light
in their digestive fireplaces
                              what your prune liver
makes them shit   like jewels delivered to the earth
their gifts for fertilizing the dirt —

you should wonder whether your ideas
of beauty are as generous.

luxe: coming issue

*

We are planning a banquet opening of our
masterpiece built on this lip of the abyss,
the ocean underclass eating below
at the base,   the rising level of the deep

swelled in turn out   to see   living high
on inheritance pending appraisal,
perilousness come of securities,
what facility comes to,   privation come of what?

The ash of the future world even now
on my fingertips should I try to lift
anything from its illustriously handed-
down table   its history   its beauty board,

shall I be the one to have to answer —
the house already up in smoke   the toast   to my Midas touch.

once the magnolia has blossomed

*

Once the magnolia blossoms,
the descending shadow of the petals
stains the street

with the brown footprint leaving,
where it has stepped in itself,

a track
walked in its own being flesh
gone as to excrement —

spring, in tomorrow's rain, comes,
a hose-down of the scene as
of an annual
                murder,

the fallen   petal
    of a sparrow

no one had kept an eye on except
the peregrine
    from the Methodist church tower.

A hose-down   as hope
this has to do with something

about the plant cycle
    of sublime season done   not sacrifice

to some stoned possession   for blood
spent on the street,

    and so much lost   you'd think
beauty had left a lesson
      more   than more is there   to ask for.

falling stars upon which to wish

*

For a brief moment in the stroke of their wings
The pale grey of their feathers turns blue

See them from above go by about two floors below
The regular brevity of that blueness makes them glow

A smoother meteor trail than lightning bugs' —
I am too silenced to wish

On   too calmed by it
What could I want?

for Salvador

distant nearness of gravity

*

A ground heat lifts the distant
mountains off the horizon;

water   absent of surface as the sky
    is   on the ground,   and like water, silvers

the air;   the movement of legs stretched
                                into sticks float
on their reflection;
                    elephants up to the sun.

All this   you've seen before
    doesn't look out of place

the same   placed in words,   until
    somewhere out there one grain

    of sand   takes on collapse black hole density
of the entire

    desert   & you feel seated   next to it.
                                    at your elbow
held to   the sun.

the glorious revolution of bouquets

*

Sparkling white   lines of block ice
float   a stiff order of wave
on the lake's opening blue   surface.

The first naval forces of spring
land   and disappear into the countryside,
to reappear   only once they've taken over,

the blossom crested
furrows of the garden
as ground water,

the resurgent uprisings stood up
against a sky
whose infiltration as

rain has betrayed the dirt
to the glorious bouquets of the order's harvest.

SurFace

*

A sphere has no face to hold it
in place   it's hard to
level.

That cannonball
weighing at your chest has got to move
one way or the other, in or out —   Your bull's eye

a fuse is almost down
to breathe or not
and who

/what   do you see in it?
This ball of air
and fractal mists

you stare into to base   something that
diverges from its line to closing on itself

picture . . .

*

. . . the shawl of rock wrapped tightly around
the emptied shoulder of a river; a canyon,
drafty bone of the ancient water woman.

Chromatic threads of sedimented layers
spun through with the mountain's mineral veins
weave into a wall   tapestry

the work of eons, the water-
shuttle   down and back into the sky, tints grain
by grain   the weft of moment bound in

the warp of day to night, light's rocking loom.
The thunder of its irregular foot
beating the floor against the slight taken, and at
its most hurt, the staggering tornado:

the drunken old ones, the earth.   For them
it hasn't gone well,   forgotten
by their children. They sell calendars.

round
*

wind erosion
blasted and burnished
on all sides

while water erosion's flow
has a direction
written in

movement
place and plasticity   directed
over millions

of years
of tiny grain arrangement
sculpture   of sediment a

long art long
art

wave ravine

*

The hunkered down round wind
eroded stone is not what water does
taking off

downstream missing
written in
sweeping hollows

the absence
as if
inhaled

and
passed out   unmolds
the abstract of

loss
it waves

but waves such as turn
heart muscle into liquid
drum

the surface
to flamenco skirt ruffle
twirling

striated frieze
spasms
of   pain against a sky usually horizoned

only with a line
This flow floods deep
into

the carved print
circuitry of concussion's phosphene stars.

levitations into air

Little mushroom size clouds of dust bellow up
through the floorboard's moves and cracking earth,

through the smeared backlight,   shelf dust pours
in sheet-like falls   off the layered cliffs of cabinet,

painted houses on souvenir cups
and saucers are swept over   right behind.

The room inside all this room
of a house inside all outdoors is

all but shaken to   and buried in its ground
is in telescopic collapse.   The idea

of a base   thrust suspended up   rapidly slamming back
too hard to balance   crushes up into down.

Our muscular body adjustments   we never noticed smooth
our movements.   in that earthquake   time —   age into tremor.

Once on the glacier, two blocks of ice the size
of houses   moved as much   as I could

hear them grind up through my teeth,
me between them on belay.   Then down in town again

on a street only wide enough for a bus and a line
of pedestrians backed against the buildings'

walls of all different soft colorings   the tiles
went flying from a couple roofs.   Otherwise,

all I noticed was a slight altitude dizziness
I took for a swagger   of having made the summit

and back.   Years later, pictures of the town
covered deep as the cross atop the cathedral

sticking knee high out of the devastatingly deep slide debris —
I think Ivan took them when he went back   last I heard   of him.

the dot flashes

. a plasma electrostatic discharge
may appear in areas above

a geologic fault as glowing lights
in the air

. angels were said to have been seen in the streets
the night before

The dots are where earthquakes have occurred
over a recorded time.   Their point

edits the map, buries it   even here
on paper,

each pepper seed spot   a mountain
of shaking, many atop another

Fire lays its own coast   lines   different
than water   its waves are vertical,

its surf a cloud of smoke and dust landing
outright   is the soil

Where we salvage the hot bricks is where
we lay them down   This flow is a march
And its again is   compacting a foundation
of coming back.

                    we don't settle very far
                    ever from our ruin

                    the soil of the fire
                    grows the best grapes

74 *

covenant

maybe the birds abandon oblivion
in need of each new forgetting

their lives —   or are skipping stones
drawing the stones to lift themselves

each throw   a line
of the splash-winged flock returning

the dots signed
the diminishing arches of rainbow

settle —   with water.
our turn if to destroy creation

settles into water our turn whether
to regret creation.

our flood is maybe thrown to skate
the surface   to the opposite bank already afire.

closer

*

The sharp knee-deep cut of the snow blower
                    is still banked on either side,
but I am walking up a shallow brook
                    of clear runoff
in the path
        water sparkling in the sunlight, shining pebbles,
and brilliant decay of leaves beneath its surface
                    stuck to the concrete.

Glacial morning   The flash thaw
        after last night's blizzard thunder and lightning
echoes with tiny chimes of melting
                    icicles   fragile as feathers
                    in their sound
heard cardinal red clear
                against the snow-light
                            branch to branch.

The birds sent after the flood   are here   in the light.
        Crow's silver brings back a pebble, a mud of blood;
the blizzard camouflaged dove, its branch of urban olive.

    A few sounds above absolute silence,
this still part hush, transparent as light,
                barely parts the morning air to speak —

this light
            pushes upstream.   Some days are closer
to the in the beginning than others.

runoff

*

You won't see it sidewinder-lap itself,
nor slither through natural gulches leaving
its city.   In flatland,
a transportation-sink channels its runoff
in planned dry beds, the El's iron aqueducts
or underground.
You see it shoot the chute down a track,

a ruling,
of straightedge waves, ties
without curl ups on the bank to sun.

From the only prairie aeries, the high rise
balconies, you'll see
the old reptilian shape shifter
scratch the day off on the city,
evolve its bird and leave

what's shed, as the trains lit windows
give it glowing new scales —
where inside, from an inside deeper
inside than what a stare
takes up,

a leaned-on dark takes up the night
with its own reflection,
in the window,
journey's oldest conversation headed
where

ice man

He had been riding a glacier. He got off
where the sun lets ice off into air.
He and the past are arriving back.
The atmosphere takes its long cooped up gasses
in again from what they've been, not as
prodigal, a different state.   Who has come
to meet him, he'd wonder if he could
and what he looked like, a past coming to them . . .
Not all stops are transfers. Was he home?

How much   is just a ride, a means
of arrival, the moving hot spot that brings
island after island to Hawaii,
the lift of peaks down along Cook Inlet,
the lava of ironworking carrying
the El, the A train, the crowd of transit
authorities and transit systems to drop you off
on the Moon, the full moon of State Street.
Or Main.   The know-how we ride without knowing.

defer to like

*

Wired to prefer ourselves   like ourselves —
But we know so little of that
possibility   so we know so little.
only the few   problems solutions we act
out of every day   and of those
only our local circumstance —

Is there water   how long before we get to it
has nothing poisoned   what I must drink —
is there a safe place to close my eyes
can I be comfortable enough I'll wake
to get some sleep —   Or if none of this
is anything I have to think   then what

do I think about instead
after I've thrown away a half-finished
ice-cold draft from the door not even needing
to be opened   of my own refrigerator
in the desert-wide of a kitchen   air
conditioned —

problems. solutions. actions.   experience
conditions   say   — how many water bottles
to carry for how far —   But reflection
on another's thirst   who has no well
from which to fill the jar of being emptied
from his home —

in the way that it gives me his thirst
deepens   say — what thirst is   to be filled.
Water never tasted the same after
that for some of us   it was as mouthing
our own tears   which welled the spring from
further   from more   there.

That kind of deference can save
some for others   the extension of tongue
from the line of snake   of jaguar
that as we sleep walks by us to the stream
walks back   by us sniffs   and doesn't eat
the sleepers —   no longer thirsty

for them.
The extension of tongue into a likeness
gives life that slakes death
the non-iterate word   between   same.
Does the grass say to the cat   you
need to eat me   by its smell the way

it talks sex to its pollinators —
because it knows everything's hunger
like its own   to live.

But when life prefers only like its own
should live
a different hunger   infects everything.

to prefer its own like rather than defer
to the like in all.

moon jar, century unclear

*

Part of the pearlescent surface is gone
from the glass back to sand,   a label
of time, that through the losses narrowing
this one from the Phoenician through the hour

glass's opening to here,   names this crust —
Only in number grains of year, not the shift,
not the heat, the fires, the person of each
who held it through, held the jar against its slake,

archeological glass breaks itself
down   from the outer layers inward into —
Feel the sandstorm of the glass dissolution
on the surface, the gritty cloud rise

out of the smooth, and transparence fade
in and out of its crust, a moon through the clouds.

to Frank Dougherty, *NY Times* photographer

the times

*

. . . stringers, freelancers, out stationed and all
others assigned were posted in an open room
off a hall that ran the length of the building
he said, he wasn't sure he even heard

the bomb go off, but he felt the floor tilt
as one slab down, one end of the structure gone
it was more a skid than being thrown, a drag
down   the hall closing behind him   and dropped

two floors outside still holding on   to his camera
in a light shower . . .   I took him to a movie   once the *Times*
reassigned him stateside   and in the preview
of upcoming features it was nothing and

he screamed and slid beneath the theater seats . . .
when I said   it's ok it's ok   I was talking . . .

to the spectators.   I heard I wasn't talking
to him   What I heard
was that silence after the explosion
redefines all sound.

I wasn't sure I even heard
when *I'd* heard it, but I felt the floor
of the same pitch
and of   something saying it's ok it's ok

more as a silence than a statement.
I realized there was hearing. *ergo sum* though it was silence
and what heard meant from there
has somehow always said.

the silence in living . . . a drop of water yet to hit the ground
the bell sound of rain in the empty sky.

acknowledgments

This work was supported in part by a
John Simon Guggenheim Memorial Foundation
fellowship (2016-2017).

I am grateful to my literary assistant, Andrew Peart,
for his help in preparing the manuscript of this book,
and to Patricia Sawzik, who gets things done.

about the author

ED ROBERSON is the author of ten previous books
of poetry, including the Los Angeles Times Book Award
finalist and Kingsley-Tufts Award runner-up *To See the
Earth before the End of the World* (Wesleyan University
Press, 2010). A former special programs administrator
at Rutgers University's Cook Campus, Roberson has
lived in Chicago since 2004 and is an emeritus professor
in Northwestern University's MFA in creative writing
program. He has also held posts at the University of
Chicago, Columbia College, the University of California,
Berkeley, and the Cave Canem retreat for Black writers.
His honors include the Jackson Poetry Prize, the Shelley
Memorial Award, the Ruth Lilly Poetry Prize, the Lila
Wallace-Reader's Digest Writers' Award, and the
African American Literature and Culture Association's
Stephen Henderson Critics Award. Born and raised
in Pittsburgh, Roberson has worked as a limnologist
(conducting research on inland and coastal fresh water
systems in Alaska's Aleutian Islands and in Bermuda),
as a diver for the Pittsburgh Aquazoo, in an advertising
graphics agency, and in the Pittsburgh steel mills. As an
expedition member of the Explorers Club of Pittsburgh,
Roberson climbed mountains in the Peruvian and
Ecuadorian Andes. He has motorcycled across the
United States and has traveled in West Africa, Mexico,
and the Caribbean.